My Life,
My Time

D.M.

Michael Terence
Publishing

First published in paperback by
Michael Terence Publishing in 2020
www.mtp.agency

ISBN 9781913653460

Dedications to...

Someone Cares in North Shields, a non-profit charity that helps people who have been sexually abused or suffered domestic abuse. They have been there for me through the bad times especially my Councillor, Donna for getting me to understand what happened to me and helping me to find out who I am.

My Care Coordinator, Helen for helping me stay in the here and now.

My good friend, Anna and her family for being there in my darkest days.

To all the District Nurses and GPs that have cared for me with my health.

If it wasn't for these people I wouldn't be here today.

Thank you. Love yous all.

- D.M. -

Contents

Introduction

Hello, my name is D.M. and I've written these poems to try and help people understand. What it can feel like when you go through childhood abuse.

When I was 11 years old, I was abused by one of my siblings. By the time I was 12 and a half I was being abused by my two siblings. By the time I was a little over 13, it was over as I thought. That was until I was 14 years when it happened again. This time I retaliated.

My family didn't know this until I spoke to people in my early 20s. That's when I told my mother who then went on to tell my father. I didn't tell them everything as I knew they were upset and the whole truth would've hurt them even more.

I locked it away until I was referred to a counsellor at Talking Therapies. They opened that box after asking a lot of questions. Then I was told they couldn't help me as in my case it was for abuse.

I then got the Someone Cares number and have been going there for a while. There I opened up to the counsellor.

I have a lot of nightmares and flashbacks and suicidal thoughts. I self-harm. Some days are worse than others.

Please read these poems and get as much help as possible before it takes complete hold of your life.

My Time

This is my time to Inspire

This is my time to Think

This is my time to Work

This is my time to Befriend

This is my time to Enjoy

This is my time to Accomplish

This is my time to Adore

This is my time to Care

This is my time to Dream

This is my time to Live

Silence

My face is puffy and red.

While the painful tears run down my eyes,
I cry out loud hoping they hear my silent screams,
so many things going through my head,
telling me I'd be better off dead.

My shaking hands over my ears trying not to listen.
I try to yell again, no-one cares
the clock is ticking by.
My body is shaking uncontrollably,
which I can't stop.

No-one cares I feel so alone and helpless,
I've come to a decision.
There's only one thing left.
I close my eyes and pray to God.

I'm so tired the pain inside won't go away.

I can no longer cry
as my eyes hurt so much.

The voices won't go away,
my heart is aching and it's unbearable for me.

No-one loves me, no-one cares no-one wants me,
I'm just not good enough.

All I ask for is that someone does care,
am I asking too much

Am so sorry, I have to end it now,
I open my eyes for the last time.

I quickly grab the razor blade,
I force the blade against my wrist.

I start to slit my veins deeper and deeper into my flesh.

Blood pours out more and more onto the floor.

I'm getting weaker and weaker,
unconscious by the seconds.

I drop the blade,
my final resting place, my bedroom floor.

My pain slowly begins to fade away with my soul.

I lay there dead, free of pain, it's quiet,
no screams, no tears, no suffering.

(Just silence)

Head High

I hold my head high. taking my power back.

He took my dignity, he took my virginity.
He stole my trust for him, he stole my trust for others.
He took my childhood away.

I hold my head high, taking my power back.

I said no, he said yes.
He made me a victim, he said I was his.

I hold my head high, taking my power back.

He said I wanted it, he said no-one would believe me.
He said they would say I lied.

I hold my head high, taking my power back.

I let him do this, I would hide, I would try to scream,
I didn't want this.

I hold my head high, taking my power back.

I'm a coward, I've learned to hate people.
I've learned to be alone, I've learned to put up a wall.

I hold my head high, taking my power back.

I'm a woman, not a child.

I try not to be a victim.

I'm trying not to be silent.

I'm holding my head high.

I'm trying to take the power back.

I Tried

I tried to find happiness,
but life gave me moments of sadness.

I tried to be strong,
but life gave me more tough times.

I tried to be normal in all situations,
but life made me abnormal.

I tried to fight back,
but life gave me criticism.

I tried to love,
but life gave me hate.

I tried to be successful,
but life gave me failure.

Oh, life,
I am just tired.

Closed My Eyes

I've closed my eyes, tears crawl down my face.

I take another drink from the vodka bottle.

My cigarette burns away.

I can no longer feel.

I see scratches and dried blood.

I shove more pills down my throat with more drink.

My body is broken.

I've completely lost my mind.

You're heavier and stronger than me.

I've fought and cried.

My head has gone blank.

I've woken to an empty bottle of pills.

And an empty bottle of vodka.

The room is spinning razor to my wrist.

I rip it across my skin.

Blood on the floor everything going black.

Cigarette burnt out.

White paper with bloodstains.

The note saying, “I’M SORRY”.

I Cannot Hide

I cannot hide.

Ugliness displayed

Shattered life never ends.

Brokenness written upon flesh.

Ashamed of scars.

Raging battle in my mind.

Screaming lay down the knife.

Weakness falling again.

As another scar appears.

Bottled up tears releasing.

Washing over my wrists.

Desperate to end this.

Battle painfully lost.

Then it starts again.

Another cut spills more.

“SHAME”

Compassion

Compassion hurts.

When I feel connected to.

Everything I also feel responsible.

For everything.

I cannot turn away.

Destiny is bound.

The destinies of others.

I must either learn to carry.

The universe or be crushed by it.

I grow strong enough.

Yet empty enough to sit down.

At the same table with the worst.

NIGHTMARES

The Urges

The urges come back.

I'm feeling the darkness.

Consuming me again.

It hurts.

I thought I would beat it this time.

But I didn't.

I'm not strong enough.

I never was.

I slide a blade.

Through my skin again.

What scares me the most.

Is it feels much better than before.

Every Day

Every day as evening comes.

The ache comes into my chest.

I know I must go to bed.

I try to sleep.

I hug my pillow close.

There's no-one around.

I cry for the things they did.

I scream without a sound.

People see me in the day.

And think am doing fine.

But every day as evening comes.

I enter my own hell.

I haven't healed my pain.

Or quietened my fears.

So every night I'm in bed.

I cry those silent tears.

Anger

There is plenty of anger in me.

It has to stop.

Why so much anger in me?

Anger is part of my frustration.

I try to control it.

Anger causes me trouble.

There is plenty of anger in me.

Do I know what anger is?

Anger is strong, feeling of loss.

Grief inside me.

Can I control it?

This triggers my anger.

Do I recognize it?

Wall

I punched the wall today.

I was so angry with myself.

My temper got the better of me.

I lost the reasons to live.

I'm never proud of anything I do.

Which makes me more frustrated.

I feel like giving up.

My anger is well alight.

The frustration is burnt out.

The blindness comes.

That's the end of me.

Ignored

I ask a question which falls flat.

I feel ignored.

Swept under the carpet.

I feel ignored.

Words disappear to my acknowledgement.

I feel ignored.

I have so many reasons to feel frustrated.

When that turns to anger.

It makes me never to return.

Believe

Believe in myself.

Though impossible it may seem.

One day, somehow, I will get this.

My goal is in view.

Am sweeping obstacles away.

Believe in myself is my plan.

Say no, I can't, but I can.

The price of life, if I win.

As I have power within.

Happiness

They say happiness will find me.

I think sadness finds me first.

It sneaks up on me in the darkness.

When I think I've made it through.

It opens a hole in solid ground.

I kind of never knew where they were.

Until I take another step.

I find myself standing over air.

The world passes me by.

Colours and sounds are a blur.

Nothing around me making sense.

I continue to plummet down.

I can't remember how it starts.

I don't know when it will end.

I know I'd give anything to stand on my feet again.

The feeling of sadness, the falling doesn't stop.

My life of meaning is sapped away.

The good things I have, then it's finally gone.

I look at the sky, it seems far away.

The one thing I have left is to cry.

People are shouting save yourself.

"Happiness and hope"

They're too busy with their own lives.

That they don't realise if they let the rope down.

It would be much easier. And a lot quicker.

The Voices

The voices in my head are telling me to kill myself.

Suicide I think is a way forward.

Am so tired of everything that's happening to me.

The voices in my head trying to get me to do it.

I refuse to let them win.

I open up to people, I cry.

I want to scream when I say these things.

Am trying to beat the voices.

I am fighting the urges.

I still need help so I can beat this thing in my head.

Describe

How to describe.

The way the knife feels.

It's slick like my skin.

Of the dozen I choose.

It's painful at first.

It will get better.

What I don't feel is my arm.

Getting wetter and wetter.

The knife runs along my flesh.

Are wait I see the mistake I have made.

Cutting today the lines are straight.

Their own batch along my arm.

How do I tell people what I do?

Or do I pass it off as a dog or cat scratch.

Trapped

Trapped in a place, theres no way out,
time stands still.

Anger all around me my voice unheard.

Theres no way out of this misery.

I am suffocating inside, the end of the maze seems
to be nowhere.

I cannot scream, I cannot cry,
I shout but it's silent.

The truth spits fire, rage,
it's burning and scolding me.

I am supposed to grow.

I've allowed myself to be Worthless, Useless, Ugly.

I have to come out of the box.

To be truthful to myself.

I cannot keep running away from this and the reality.

I must stand and see the truth.

Instead of dodging it.

I have to face the truth of what they did.

The Urges

The urges come back.

I'm feeling the darkness.

Consuming me again.

It hurts.

I thought I would beat it this time.

But I didn't.

I'm not strong enough.

I never was.

I slide a blade.

Through my skin again.

What scares me the most.

Is it feels much better than before.

Hold on

Hold on, hold on.

By tomorrow this will be done.

Hold your head up high.

Let these memories pass me by.

Go on finish that letter.

I am stronger than I think.

Go on cry, it's better than being crushed.

Stand back up if I fall.

It doesn't matter if I crawl.

Go ahead crawl away.

I will pick myself up.

I am a fighter.

In the dark, I burn brighter.

So hold my head up high.

Keep my eyes on the prize.

I Am the Author

I am the author of my life.
So if I feel I can't cope.
Don't put a full stop on it.
Battle through it and hope.
I could just give up.
But instead, I fight.
Battle in the darkness.
Until I see light.
Don't leave a short story.
Words of my pain.
The story of strength.
And the things I can gain.
Take the first step.
Strong in each hour.

Carry on my story.

Be proud of my power.

Who Would Miss Me?

Depression isn't obvious.

But to me suicide is.

I've said I'd do it one day.

Because the pain and memories aren't always clear.

No-one can deny it when they find my body.

They will see depression isn't clear.

My body floats in the air.

Tumbling to my death.

Will they realise the pain is real.

Will they know the pain is real.

In my heart and head.

Would they care.

After all who would miss me.

I Know

I know sometimes.

I feel like nobody cares.

I can hardly call my home a home.

I do what I have to.

But it always ends in tears.

If I told you losing is my biggest fear.

That there is someone who cares.

I want to laugh, see my eyes gleam again.

Help me find the light in the dark.

When the light returns.

I hear the noises within my soul.

This Is Me

Am sad.

Am hurt.

Am dying.

Am alone.

Am lonely.

Am a mess.

Am judged.

Am ignored.

Am suicidal.

Am confused.

Am depressed.

Am misunderstood.

Am tired, but living.

Am hurt, but don't show it.

Am screaming, but silent.

Am in pain, but still smiling.

"This is me."

The Urges

The urges come back.

I'm feeling the darkness.

Consuming me again.

It hurts.

I thought I would beat it this time.

But I didn't.

I am not strong enough.

I never was.

I slide a blade.

Through my skin again.

What scares me the most.

Is it feels much better than before.

Am I Brave?

I think am brave to get up in the morning.
Even if my soul is weary and my bones ache for a rest.

I think am brave that I keep on living.
Even if I don't know how anymore.

I think am brave that I push away the tears.
Rolling down my face every day and I fight it daily.

I know there are days when I feel like giving up.
But I think am brave that I never do.

One Day / No Help

I am walking down the street.
I fall into a black hole.
I try to get out, there's no help.

Next day.

I am walking down the street.
I fall again into this black hole.
There's a box to help me out,
but still I can't get out.

Next day.

I am walking down the street.
I fall again into this black hole.
There's another box so I put the two together and
try to get out.

Next day.

I am walking down the street.
I fall again into this black hole,
there are some step ladders.
I climb the ladders, I get out of the black hole.
It's much easier this time.

Next day.

I am walking down the street.
I don't fall this time into the black hole.
I start to laugh, I thank god it didn't happen again.
I am though the worse of it.

"Moral of the story"
"how did I get out the black hole in the first place"

(no such place as a black hole)

Darkness

Days are black.
Lying behind.
The golden sun.
It blinds me.

My thoughts are black.
Wandering around my head.
I cannot connect the dots.
Good or bad.

The world is black.
It's pitch dark outside.
Swirling around.
Nowhere to hide.

It remains black.
Am fighting no more.
Dark it is.
Behind the black door.

It's Getting Late

When it's late, am getting tired.

Darkness rises in me.

Distractions are gone.

My confidence disappears.

Fading silence rises in me.

I lay down my head.

And slowly drift away.

Doubt will visit.

Fear rises in me.

When memories are close.

The terror begins.

I will have to fight till it breaks me.

Demons inside me, when night falls.

What scares me is not the darkness outside.

It's being alone with those thoughts.

It's darkness inside me.

Hatred

Hatred grows towards me the pain in my heart
grows stronger.
I wish to end my life.

That knife placed on the table.
Forgive me if I use the knife to end my life.

The pain in my heart is just too much.
I've stopped myself doing it.

That knife, thinking of how and when to do it.
How my friends would feel if I left them.

Why can't death be simple?
To choose when to die.

Locked

Locked within my mind.

Unable to escape.

Reaching for help.

It’s not there.

Demons inside.

No-one can save me.

So tired of struggling to no avail.

Exhausted and worn out.

Screaming let me out.

He Hurt Me.

I am upset.

I don't want to go on.

I want to die.

He hurt me.

He made me cry.

He called me names.

He hurt me.

I was at home (safe).

He abused me.

He frightened me.

He scared me.

He hurt me.

I didn't tell.

I was upset.

I was quiet.

I wanted to scream.

He hurt me.

The hurt was pain.

I felt trapped.

I can't cope.

Am on my own.

He hurt me.

I went to bed, I cried all night.

Same every night, until I die.

He hurt me.

Everybody

Everybody says time will heal.

Everybody says talking helps.

Everybody says writing helps.

Everybody says you're safe.

Everybody says it can't happen again.

Everybody says he can't reach you.

Everybody says relax.

Everybody says be happy.

Everybody says the fear will go away.

Everybody doesn't know this

Everybody doesn't know he never leaves my mind.

Everybody doesn't know it reminds me every day.

My Day

My day.

Is ash grey.

My night's too long.

My words are wrong.

Nothing good to say.

I rest, my dreams come.

Not for the best.

A long night ahead.

Daylight comes.

With boredom too.

Why do I bother?

To get up so soon.

Could this be a good day?

The Pain

The pain inside.

Where no-one can see.

Is slowly killing me.

The thoughts inside.

Are ripping me apart.

There haunting me.

So dark it hurts so badly.

The scars outside.

Are just marks.

From wounds within.

Sound and Look

You can sound confident.

But have anxiety.

You can look healthy.

But still feel ill.

You can look happy.

But be miserable inside.

You can be good looking.

But still feel ugly.

So be kind because every person.

Is fighting a battle.

We know nothing about them.

Familiar

Familiar place another night's dream.

Fluttering in dusty light.

A life so long, but to short.

Secrets worth keeping but worth telling.

Feeling so solid but liquefied.

Pure but so strong in a woman's eyes.

Feeling alone and being alone.

I quiver and sigh, silent in the night.

It falls deeper and deeper.

The terror takes over, I'll be fine.

I'll be okay, don't mind me.

As I slip away into the darkness.

Don't Quit

When things go wrong as they always do.

When the road I'm trudging is all uphill.

When my funds are low and debts are high.

I want to smile but just sigh.

The care is pressing me down.

I have to rest, but don't want to quit.

Life is twists and turns.

As everyone sometimes learns.

Many a failure turns.

When I might have won if I'd stuck it out.

Don't give up the pace as it seems slow.

I may succeed with a blow.

Success is failure inside and out.

Clouds of doubt.

I never can tell how close I am.

So I stick to the fight as I'm harder to hit.

When things seem wrong.

"I must not quit."

Guilty

I feel guilty for everything even if am not involved.

I've got no control over any situation.

I feel like everything is bad.

It's occurred because of me.

It's my fault I should've seen it coming.

Even if I logically knew there was nothing I could have done.

I cannot shake the feelings of guilt.

Scared

Scared and alone the little girl cries herself to sleep.

No-one to hold her, no-one to tell, so alone.

Eleven-year-old's tears falling down her face,
so out of place.

Secrets told to her pillowcase.

They were her older siblings,
they were there to protect her.

Love her as a sister.

Parents would leave them alone.

One would find her and ruin her life,
tell her you will die if you tell anyone.

That little girl kept it a secret for many years.

The two siblings involved did so much more to her.

One after the other, time and time again.

That little girl lost her life because of them.

That little girl feels less of a person now.

That little girl is me.

What I went through as a little girl is not what families do.

I see their faces.

I'm scared in case they come after me.

Printed in Poland
by Amazon Fulfillment
Poland Sp. z o.o., Wrocław

61951376R00054